Who Am I?
African Animals

Written by Read With You
Center for Language Research and Development

Published by Read With You Publishing

Designed by Read With You Center for Language Research and Development

Read With You and associated logos are trademarks and/or registered trademarks of Read With You, LLC.

ISBN-13: 978-1-944710-71-2
ISBN-10: 1-944710-71-X

Printed in the United States of America.

I am the "king of the jungle!"

Who am I?

I am the tallest animal on earth.

Who am I?

giraffe

My stripes help me hide.

Who am I?

I am the largest land animal.

Who am I?

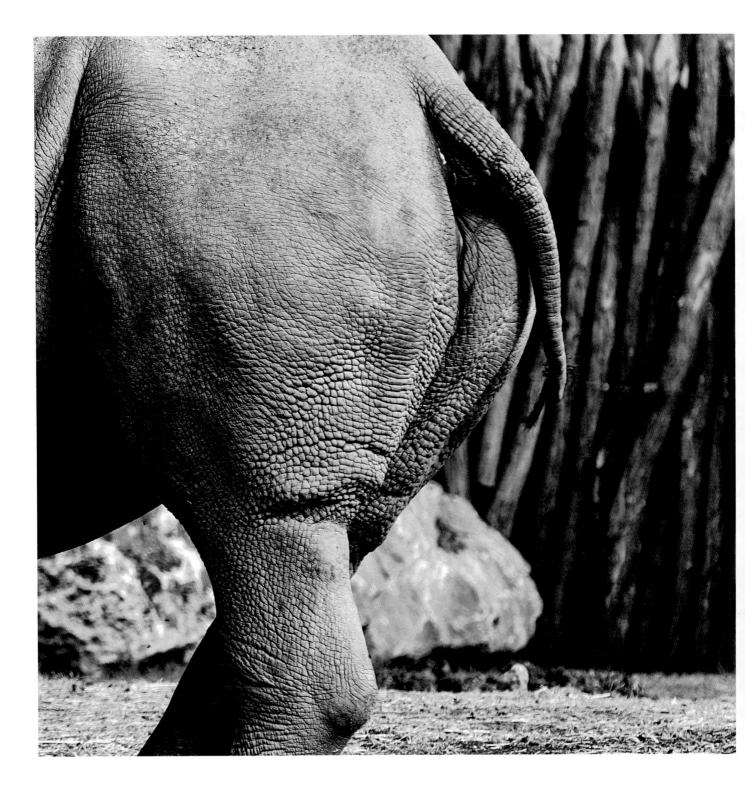

I have a horn on my nose.

Who am I?

I can run, swim, and climb.

Who am I?

leopard

I eat dead animals.

Who am I?

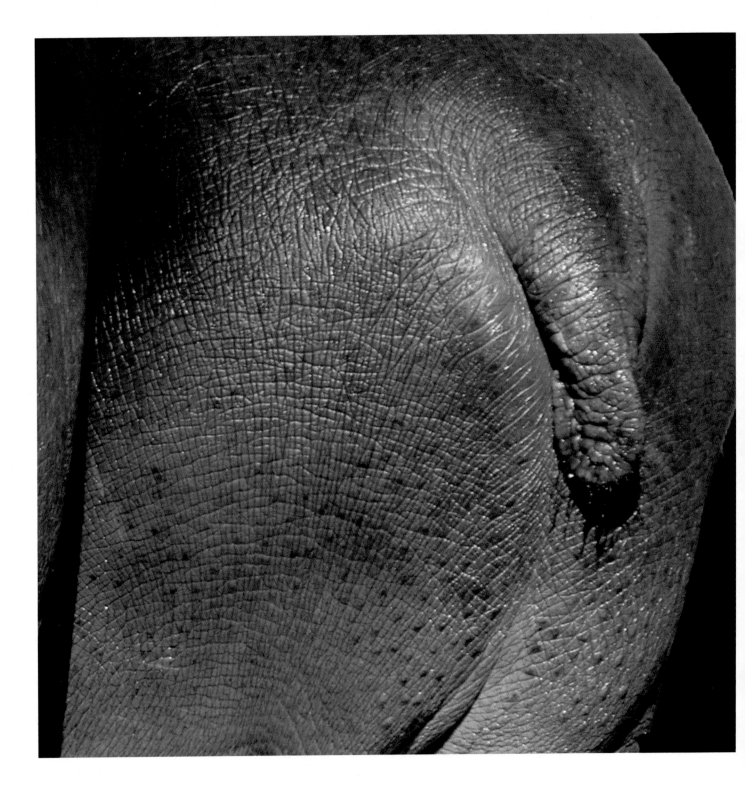

I can close my nostrils and ears.

Who am I?

Giraffe

Zebra

Lion

Elephant

I am a lion.

I am a giraffe.

I am a zebra.

I am an elephant.

We are African animals.

Rhino

Vulture

Leopard

Hippopotamus

I am a rhino.

I am a vulture.

I am a leopard.

I am a hippopotamus.

We live on African plains.

Plains are open, flat spaces with lots grass or grasslike vegetation.

Made in the USA
Monee, IL
19 March 2023

30216380R00017